Soul Musings

Dr. Sujatha Nair

BookLeaf Publishing

India | USA | UK

Made with ❤ on the BookLeaf Publishing Platform
www.bookleafpub.in
www.bookleafpub.com

Acknowledgement

To all the fantastic humans and non- humans in my life who have dedicated their lives to facilitate people to take the reins of their lives into their own able hands.
My parents, my sister Sushma, my brother, Shashi, and Divi—to whom I am always Chits—my family.

To Mahesh Hiranandani, Dr. Prabhakar Devadiga, Dr. Rajiv Jerajani, Dr. Shashi Menon, Vandana Hiranandani, Rajan Pillay Farhang and Dr. Chintan Dalal—my beloveds, mentors, and gurus.
All my clients and patients - each of whom I have only learnt from.

To my Anatta Family.

To my dearest friends—Sonal Kudtarkar, Dr.Sonali Mahale, Dr. Dipika Mitra, Dr. Farhin Katge, and Shanti Nair—to name the closest and the many who know they are close to my heart.

To the numerous cats who have come into my life—great therapists, every one of them—and the current Isis of my heart.

Preface

Soul Musings is a collection of impromptu poems, each reflecting different periods and experiences of my life. With gratitude, I share them with you.

Prisoners of the Mind

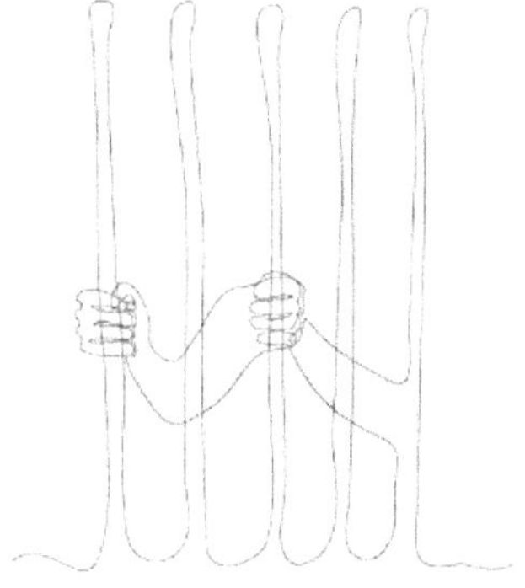

Beings of the world,
Closed to new experiences, new possibilities,
Leading to undiscovered potentialities
All because we are prisoners of our own
minds.
Limitless are we,
Limited by our thoughts
Trapped in the vortices of our mind
Imprisoned, by our own selves.

Beyond Judgements

Beaten and battered am I,
Entangled in the chains of so-called
self-respect and personal ethics.
Who am I to impose them upon others?
Who am I to judge, to punish, to demean?
To tolerate, or, not tolerate,
To raise up on a pedestal or pull down to the
dredges?
Each to his own—
Loving and living.

Moments

An opportunity seized,
Time freed from the humdrum of life,
Those stolen moments—
A hidden smile,
A snatched kiss,
Keeps our love afresh and alive!

On The Threshold

I am living on the threshold of this house,
As though within a golden womb,
Waiting to be born.
I am the midwife, I am the newborn,
Look at this conflict.
I am living on the threshold of this house.

If

If I could wrap this fragrant air and send you,
If I could get you to feel the softness of this
sand, beneath your feet,
If I could make you experience the divinity
here,
If I could get nature to envelop you,
If I could direct the winds of the river and the
sea to caress you,
Oh My Love, If I could curate a bouquet of all
these for you...

Ode to Isis

Isis, mine—no less than an Egyptian goddess
are you.
You entered my porch at a month and three,
A black, white, and orange calico beauty.
Captured me, hook, line, and sinker did thee.
The couch—your home, your sanctuary,
Therapeutic to many, by your quiet, silent,
soft presence,
Speaking through your eyes, you seek me out.

As a mater, you transformed
into a fierce, protective being.
I saw a side both loving and giving.
3 times you bred,
lost many of your brood,
grieved, yet stood by the remaining—
giver of life to all...

Isis, mine—no less than an Egyptian Goddess
are you.

Healing

Healing happens..
With an abundance of love and compassion..
First, to oneself.
The overflow then becomes an outpouring to
others!
'Til that happens, hurt people hurt others,
Healed—do you want to be? Don't dither,
feeling good or getting better, are good
benchmarks to ponder.

Halt! Stop! Look within.
What is your role in your life's meanderings?
Honestly answer, without wandering,
Shifting the strobe light, the finger, the sight,
Confronting, at last, this blithering oversight,
Healing happens—

The dams break, the walls crumble, the ego
shatters.
Light rushes through…
Healing happens..

Emotions- Veil from Reality

Emotions....
They render us selfish,
Insensitive to our own selves,
Blindsided
and blinded to the very people we claim to
love.
Emotions, a veil, that keep us from reality.

Escape we try to, through alcohol, drugs, or
sob stories,
To numb, to forget,
Neither happens however,

Neither happens however.
We numb pain, we numb joy, we numb
happiness too.
Compartmentalise, we cannot.
Emotions...
They render us selfish.

The True Constant

Legend has it,
Change is the true constant
True, really, is it?
Kaleidoscope like, the world around keeps a'
changing.
Our core, pure silence, unchanged,
unmoved..
Silence - the true constant,
permeating the core of the chaos.

Expectations

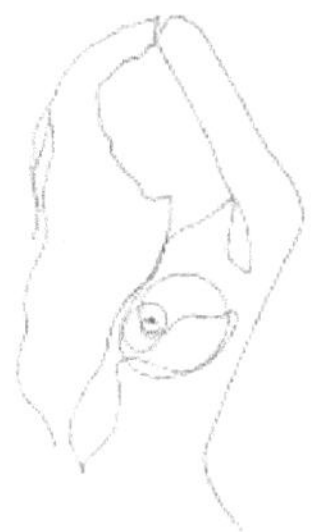

I am your son! I am your daughter!
I am your mother! I am your father!
I am your wife! I am your husband!
I am your friend!
I am You!
Expectations outpouring from all directions,
Cacophony like, deafening, engulfing ,
drowning...
Which do we fulfill, whom do we please,
Whom do we appease ?
Oh, the pain, the disappointment, the
betrayal,
The glorious advice—drop all expectations!
But,
Expecting one to drop all expectations—
—is also an expectation !
A quandary it is.

Boundless

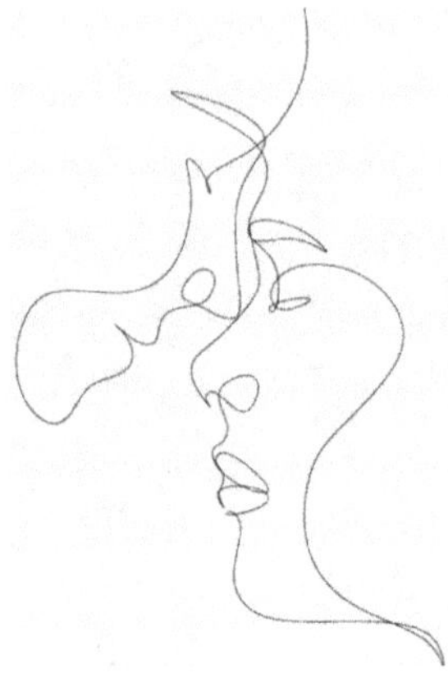

I have no boundaries with you, my beloved,
Many a time have I raised a veil,
Only for it to be rended every single time
Many a time have I endeavoured to build a
wall brick by brick,
with the cement and mortar of tears and
grief,
Mowed down was it every single time
Many a time have I enclosed my heart in iron
shackles,
Locked and thrown away the key,
Only for it to be cut open every single time,
Many a time have I built a dam around
myself,

only for it to be burst open every single time
By the force of Love for you, bursting forth
through every tear, chink, mortar and dam,
flooding everything that comes its way,
I have no boundaries with you, my Beloved,
How can I bind that which is boundless?

Me

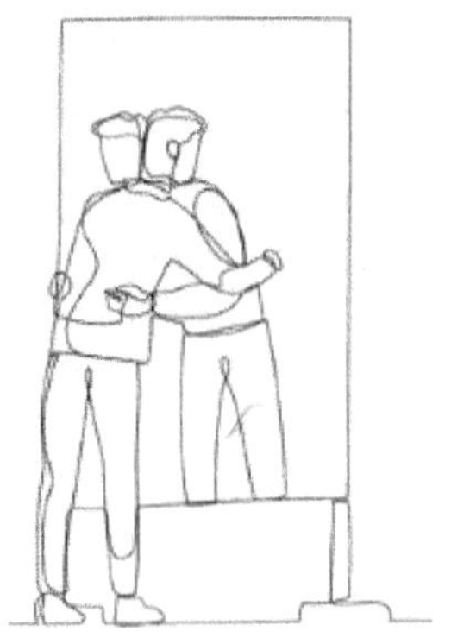

You are so good.
You are so wise.
You are so beautiful.
You are so intelligent.
You are so enlightened.
You are stupid.
You are selfish.
You are a liar.
You are bad.
You are naive.

A meagre image of others' perceptions, am I?
Or a meagre image of my own perceptions,
am I?

Let me be me—truly, unapologetically, me,
Beyond perceptions... free.

Celestial

A geo-magnetic celestial alignment,
Happening once in 144 years,
Once-in-a-lifetime phenomenon for anyone
in this world,
Except, perhaps, for the sea turtles.
Healing, spiritual, re- alignment of Self,
The Universe collaborating for the nectar of
immortality to awaken within.
A churning, chaotic, a shedding of the old
Rebirth, renewal, living the New being
Who went, who stayed behind, who returned?
Remains to be seen.

Untrodden

I have walked on paths untrodden,
Where those of my ilk dared not tread.
Watched the shackles, wrought by mine own mind
Drop away, sheared through by the gentle
light of mine own awareness.
Filled with gratitude am I, to all the hands
that held mine on this path,
Yet, I have miles to go before I hang up mine
own boots...
Yet, I have miles to go before I hang up mine
own boots...
'Til I meld with the One.

Bond

Whom do I bind,
Who binds me,
Who holds the moorings of my life?
Between bond and bondage,
Life slips by...
Let me be free of all binds,
Let me be moored in You,
Till there is no Me, no Mooring, and no You.

Chained

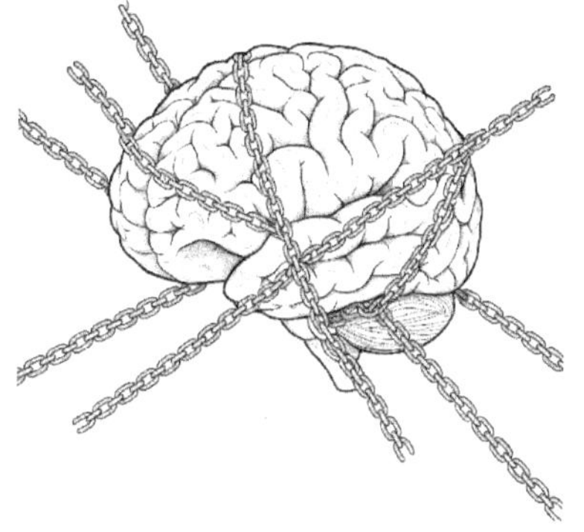

Shackle ourselves we do with the chains of
our emotions,
and pull them with our own hands,
Fall flat on our faces, do we, every single time,
and yet we look around scathingly ,
Asking pityingly," Who pulled my chain?",
"Who pulled my chain?"
'Til we look within, not scathingly,
but with love and compassion,
Voila! The chains drop away.

Growth

A rush of blood to my face,
The muscles of my temples tighten and throb.
Suddenly, I go deaf to all else being said,
Expectations—shattered once again.
All explanations, like watered-down tea,
bland, lame,
Quiet, I keep watching, reaction, spews.
Regret, not yet surfaced in the face of
pulsating anger,
I voice what I really want to say..
The pulsation dissolves, as if I am washed over
by cool water. I know, the anger was my
body's old response, pulling me back.
Voicing it, instead, freed it,

Next time, pause, breathe, voice it to the air,
Practice checks,
To jump out of old stories the body-mind
relives.
Free from old reins, evolving into Truth.

The Oak

Be like the Oak, my friend,
Roots that go as deep and far
 as its trunk, reaching high to touch the skies
Feeding and protecting generations
Flora and fauna- abound, safe, sated,
Bark, like an armour,
that protects and provides,
Fire destroys it not
Frost freezes it not
Storms uproot it not
Be like the Oak, my friend

Love

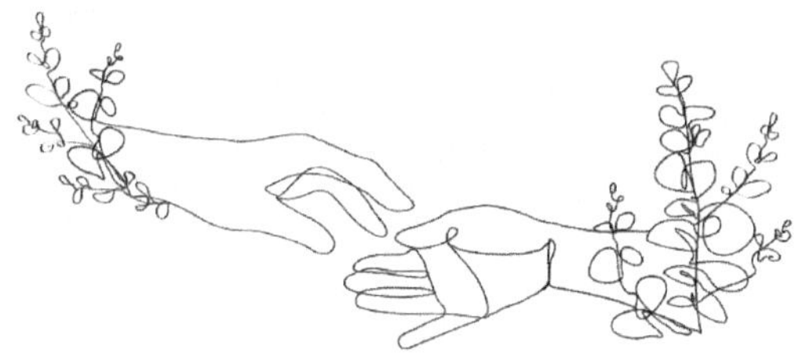

Wars have been fought over Love,
Kingdoms have been lost over Love,
Beloveds have died for their Love
An oft thrown around word
That sounds like an abuse on many a sly
tongue.

I went to Love, with my possessiveness,
jealousy, hatred, need, shame, hurt, blame,
lust,
All paraded under the guise of "Love."
Love said, "I am none of the above,
Stop maligning me with all these labels,
I don't exist in their midst."
I am Unconditional, beyond all.
I Am, Love.

Grief

He died.
It was inevitable.
He was freed, and so was she,
But bound me in a vortex.
It still seemed unreal.
I will never see him again.
I will never see his face light up like a child on
seeing me,
I will never be able to pull his long soft ear
lobes,
I will never hear his voice.

Grief arrives in many forms—
In a tone of voice heard long ago,
A whiff of food cooked by him,

dreams
memories- his smiling face etched in me.

Whom do we grieve for—the ones passed on
or for we, who remain?
We grieve for ourselves, as the loss is ours...
The eternal absence,
Like a breath half taken.

Mother Nature

The crickets crying,
chirping of birds announcing dawn,
light streaming and slowly engulfing the sky
with its hues,
birds bathing in the earthen jacuzzi,
cats rubbing themselves against me, asking
for food.
Sun birds, glittering like a kaleidoscope,
the Bharadwaj, crying its auspicious notes
flower buds blooming,
dew afresh on the leaves,
the crisp fresh morning air,
Mother Nature resplendent in all her glory,
the head bows in reverence and gratitude.